XTREME

7.99

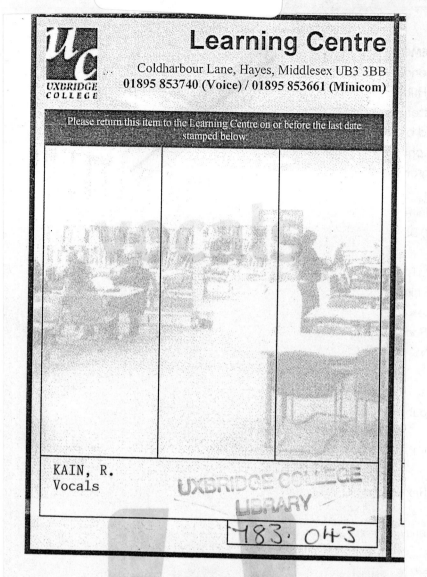

ACKNOWLEDGEMENTS

CD produced, engineered, recorded and mixed by Phil Hilborne @ WM Studios.CD compiled, mastered, edited and voiceovers recorded/mixed by Phil Hilborne @ WM Studios. www.philhilborne.com. Additional Keyboard Programming/Editing: Phil Hilborne.

Printed in the United Kingdom by
MPG Books Ltd, Bodmin

Published by SMT, an imprint of
Sanctuary Publishing Limited
Sanctuary House
45–53 Sinclair Road
London W14 0NS
United Kingdom

www.sanctuarypublishing.com

Copyright: Roger Kain, 2004

Picture Credits: Rex Features,
and Redferns
Design and Editorial: Essential Works

ISBN: 1-84492-034-8

XTREME

vocals

Roger Kain

smt

CONTENTS

MEET YOUR TUTORS: HARMONY AND KLASH

These two reprobates will take you, step by step, through the exercises, and encourage you to go for the sounds you really want to make. Pay attention to both of them; they're both right, even when they're arguing with each other.

WELCOME FROM HARMONY

'Hi! I'm Harmony, and this is to tell all you extremists what your voice is all about – well, us girls, anyway. We're the real singers! The boys can read Klash's rubbish – if he's learned to write yet! Come to that, the boys had better read this as well – they won't get much from his bit, which comes second – d'you get that? – second! After mine!'

WELCOME FROM KLASH

'Hey dudes! Welcome to all you Xtremists. You've listened to your favourite tracks with your favourite singers. Ever tried them out? Ever wondered why they can do it and you can't? Ever been told to shut up, 'cos you can't sing? We've all been told that! But have you ever thought, 'What am I doing wrong?' The answer is probably, 'Nothing'. You just haven't been shown the tricks (posh people call it 'technique') – the things to do to get the wicked sounds.'

YOUR TUTORS ARE HERE TO...

GUIDE YOU...

'When you're young, singing comes easily. That doesn't mean you can go at it like a mad thing, screaming the place down and all that. Well, not yet. You've got to do some work with your power muscles, or you'll wreck your throat. The most important power muscles for singing are called the diaphragm, or the front abdominal muscles. These muscles are in the stomach – if you want to go loud enough for attitude you have to start off from the stomach.'

'Dudes' voices change a lot between the ages of 8 and 14, so what you can sing changes a lot too. When you get to 13 or 14 your voice 'breaks'. It gets deeper and better. Now this bit's important: you can't go bashing away at your throat all the time, 'cos your throat will pack up very quickly. You have to use your power muscles – they're in your stomach, your legs and your bum.'

ADVISE YOU...

'Now, some of y'all might be able to get some deep chest sounds while you're young. You're lucky. Work at it, but don't force it. There's a big difference between working hard for something difficult – and forcing. And the difference is called 'technique'.

Most singers are shy. However Xtreme they may be on stage – it's an act. So act, dude! Don't think, 'I can't do it because I don't have any self-confidence.' Start your set with something fast, loud and (if possible) high – the punters will go wild, and you'll feel fantastic. The secret is this: when you sing you can be the person you want to be.'

TEST YOU...

'The best way to learn anything is to test yourself. Each lesson has some questions, with answers at the back of the book.

Yeah, but if you're anything like Klash, you'll probably look at the answers first!'

AND, OCCASIONALLY, TO MAKE YOU LAUGH...

'Make you laugh? I'm not a figure of fun. If you want a good laugh, listen to Klash on the CD.'

'She's got no dignity! Well, I'm not rising to it. If she wants to sound like a right divvy, that's up to her.'

YOUR INSTRUMENT

Your instrument is your body – you are your own instrument. Singing's not like playing a guitar. 'Cos when you first pick up a guitar, you start off like a beginner; but singing's different. No one's really a beginner at singing. Everyone sings, from the pram onwards. But if you want it to sound fantastic you have to practise, or you won't even be able to sing in tune. So, let's look at how it all works, taking the important parts of your body bit by bit:

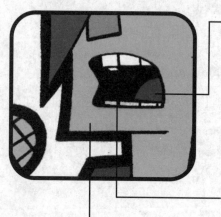

YOUR TONGUE You have to keep the tip of your tongue against your bottom teeth, or bottom gum, all the time – well, nearly all the time. This is the second most important technique in singing, almost as important as getting the jaw down. This might sound funny, but keep practising, you'll get used to it, and it makes singing much easier. A woman's tongue is stronger than a man's (well, Harmony's is!) – it's the only muscle that is, so don't let it flap around!

YOUR PALATE This is the roof of your mouth, and it's in two halves.
The hard palate This is the front half of the roof of your mouth. It stretches from the top teeth to half-way back where it meets the soft palate in a V-shaped join. It's very hard, and is sometimes called the sounding board of the voice. You focus your voice on your hard palate, but it usually feels as if you are focussing in your nose. It puts a good edge on your voice, making it much easier to sing, so that everyone says you've got a fantastic voice. The best way of focussing in the nose and on the hard palate is to push the tip of the tongue against the bottom teeth or gums.
The soft palate This is the back half of the roof of your mouth. It's a muscle, so you have to stretch it to make it work properly, like all muscles.

YOUR JAW Your jaw is the only bone in your head that moves. You have to push it down on the open sounds – 'Ah, I, all, etc…' so that your mouth is wide open, really stretched like a big yawn – or a big scream. Getting the jaw down on all the open sounds is the most important technique in singing, otherwise the jaw will lock in the half-way position, and you'll never get the really high notes or really low notes.

YOUR HEAD Your head keeps your brains warm. Generally, you're supposed to keep your head straight up and down and on the level when you're singing. Sometimes you have to put your head down a bit for tricky notes, like very high notes or very low notes. You're not supposed to let your head go backwards, except for very advanced techniques.

YOUR NECK This is the weakest part of the body. Don't put pressure on it – put the pressure on the power muscles instead. The neck includes:

The carotid arteries These are those funny thick pipes that stand out on both sides of the neck when you're doing it wrong. If they stand out on your neck it means (1) you haven't taken a big enough breath, (2) you're not supporting it enough with the stomach, and (3) you're being lazy, and we hope it hurts your head!

The larynx, sometimes called the 'voice box' This is in the front of your neck. Don't touch it; let your brain sort it out.

The vocal cords, sometimes called the 'vocal folds' These are tiny and flat. You can't see them from the outside of the neck. They move incredibly fast while you're singing, but no one knows why.

THE POWER MUSCLES Power and range do not come from the neck, they come from the power muscles, and they're all in the bottom half of the body, from the waist down, miles away from the neck. The main power muscles are:

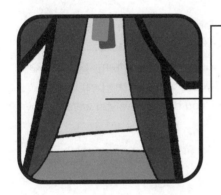

The diaphragm This muscle makes the floor of the lungs. It's shaped like a sort of hump. Singing teachers always say, 'Support the voice from the diaphragm.' But that's only half right – the diaphragm hardly does anything when you're singing. What they mean is the 'front abdominal muscles', but that's a right mouthful! That's why they go on calling it the 'diaphragm', 'cos it's easier to say. Why don't they just call it the 'stomach'? Anyway, we're supposed to tell you about the diaphragm, so we've told you.

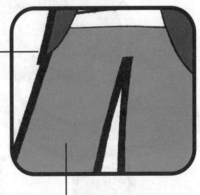

The bum Well, what else can you call it? Bottom, backside, posterior, jack, jacksy… We've decided on 'bum' – even Shakespeare uses it in *A Midsummer Night's Dream* and *Measure For Measure*. If it's good enough for Shakespeare, it's good enough for us! Well, your bum is a powerful muscle structure, but it also co-ordinates the other power muscles – it makes all the big muscles work together. You can sing with your bum in two ways. (1) Clench it – that means you squeeze your cheeks, making your bum muscles rock hard. That will give you some great high notes. (2) Push them outwards, stick your bum out and go for a fart (our teacher says 'constipate it!') – that will give you some wicked screams.

The leg muscles Your thighs are the strongest muscles you've got. So, when your voice is going ballistic and Xtreme, you'd be daft not to use them. You should feel as if you're pushing down through the floor. You'll know when you're doing this right 'cos your calf muscles will ache.

YOUR VOICE

HARMONY SAYS

Girl, your voice is really three voices: your head voice, your chest voice and your screaming voice.

HEAD VOICE This is the high falsetto voice that sounds girlie, childish and silly. A lot of classical singers sing in this voice. But it's important – incredibly important – for the rest of your voice. The head voice is the healing part. If you want to sort out your best voice you've got to sing high in exercises. You have to do the sweet, silly sounds.

CHEST VOICE This is the low, serious voice that sounds all dark and hard – the voice with attitude! You need to keep exercising the low notes – build up the deep, dark sounds or they dry up. Don't force them or you'll go out of tune. Build them up patiently. You can actually take this voice up quite high, but that takes a lot of hard work in both the head and the chest voices.

SCREAMING VOICE This is an extension of the falsetto voice. When you get to the top of the falsetto voice, scream and you can go much higher. Screaming is loud. It's the loudest sound an Xtremist can make. If you try to do it quietly you will hurt your throat. It's the best way of stretching the soft palate – that's why you did it when you were a baby.

KLASH SAYS

Dudes have four voices (one more than babes have got!): your natural head voice, falsetto head voice, chest voice and screaming.

NATURAL HEAD VOICE This is the high part of your natural voice, which some singers think is high chest voice, 'cos that's what it sounds like. It's very difficult and loud – you have to work at it – but it's where all your magical singing starts.

FALSETTO HEAD VOICE This is the high, childish voice – it sounds like crying – it can go much higher than the natural voice. It should be easy – if it's not you're doing something wrong. You've been doing this voice all your life so you should be good at it by now! This is the voice that saves you when the rest of your voice is rubbish. And that happens to all of us – you can't be good all the time! If you can get the falsetto voice working, the rest of it will start to work. My teacher says it's the healing part of your voice. If you can do the falsetto, you can join up all your voices and then it sounds fantastic, but that takes a long time. Well, what else are you gonna do for the rest of your life?

CHEST VOICE This is the low voice. If you can get it down deep enough you can do death metal, grunge, etc... This just takes work and patience. You can't force low notes or they go wrong. But they change the rest of your voice and make it all sound really serious.

SCREAMING VOICE This is the same for both dudes and babes. Sorry, guys, but you're gonna have to check out the girl's stuff above.

LESSONS

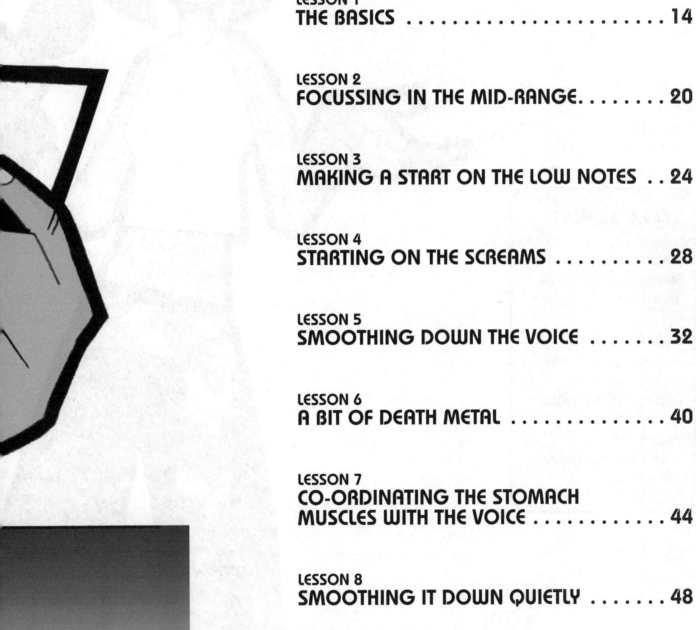

THE BASICS

Here we're gonna concentrate on breathing, the diaphragm (that's your stomach!) and a few high notes. Are you ready?!

YOUR GOALS

GOAL 1
To learn to breathe from the stomach.

GOAL 2
To start to sing from the stomach instead of singing from the throat.

GOAL 3
To sing some high notes – well difficult.

THEORY

This is singing theory, not music theory. Music theory is about chords and harmony – it's about writing music down on paper. Singing theory is about voice production – the best ways of making the sounds you want, and putting the right sort of acting into your voice for the song you're doing. Singing is mostly acting. When you're doing SKUNK ANANSIE you want one sort of sound, for Christmas carols you want another sort of sound.

EXERCISE 1a

BREATHING FROM THE STOMACH

STEP 1
Stand up. First, put your hands on your stomach and put your tongue firmly against your bottom teeth.

STEP 2
Breathe in – that means fill up your stomach with air. (Think of your stomach as a balloon. When you fill it up with air it gets bigger, when you empty it, it goes flat.)

STEP 3
Breathe out, so that your stomach gets very flat – use your hands to help push all of the air out. Fill up again... and so on.

STEP 4
Try breathing in through your nose and out through your mouth. If you can't take in enough air through your nose it doesn't matter; you can breathe in through your mouth if you have to – as long as you keep your tongue against your bottom teeth. Repeat the whole thing three or four times. If you go dizzy you're doing it right. You're probably breathing more deeply than ever before.

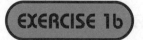

EXERCISE 1b

USING THE STOMACH FOR POWER

Now put the voice into it.

STEP 1

Fill up your stomach with air again, as in Exercise 1a.

STEP 2

Push your jaw right down as far as it will go – like a yawn – keeping your tongue against your bottom teeth all the time.

STEP 3

Now slam the stomach in hard and make the sound 'Ha!', giving it a really good 'H' from the stomach.

STEP 4

Make the sound in the nose. This is called 'focussing the voice'. You should try to avoid making the voice in the throat – always try to focus it in the nose.

YOUR GOALS

GOAL 1
To stretch the soft palate which, like any muscle, works best when it is stretched.

GOAL 2
To get over the fear of high notes.

GOAL 3
To make some wicked sounds.

THEORY

High notes are difficult, so you have to work at them. If you can't do them all straight away don't worry about it – try again tomorrow! You need to do the high notes or your voice will be dodgy and boring. (This is because high notes stretch the soft palate – that's what makes your voice sound wicked!)

EXERCISE 2

FIRST ATTEMPTS AT HIGH NOTES

STEP 1

Take a big breath – puff up the stomach – keep your tongue against your bottom teeth.

STEP 2.

When the voice goes up, pull the stomach in (or when you see this sign over a note ^). When the voice goes down, push the stomach out again.

STEP 3.

This zigzag line over a note wwwww means you should shake the voice by shaking the stomach (it's called vibrato). DON'T do it by shaking the throat or you'll reduce your range – and it will probably make you look very old while you're doing it!

PROBLEM?

High notes are frightening. The danger is that your fear will cause you to scrunch up the throat, and you'll strangle the note. Then you'll tell yourself that you can't do high notes. If it's difficult for you, do as much as you can but don't force it.

A lot of dudes can't go higher than this at first – it takes time. If you can – do it!

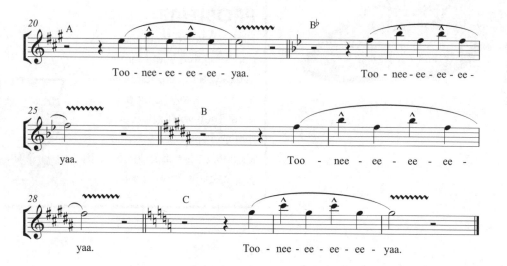

TIP

You might find the top notes hard. A lot depends on how much you really want them. Top notes are loud, if you don't go loud enough for a top A you'll never get a top A. Keep working at it. As you work through these lessons you'll get better at top notes (and bottom notes); but it takes some dudes a long time – months, even years – to be good at top notes.

PROBLEM?

The carotids (carotid arteries) might be standing out on the side of your neck; if they are, they're probably giving you quite a painful headache. If this is happening to you, you are probably not working hard enough at your technique. Take the biggest breath you can with the stomach, pull the stomach in for the top notes (marked ^ in the score), and keep your tongue against your bottom teeth.

TEST

QUESTION 1
What is the single most important technique in singing?

QUESTION 2
When you don't have to get the jaw down because it's not an open sound, what are the three essential techniques for getting high notes?

FOCUSSING IN THE MID-RANGE

This is one of those daft bits of singing that does your voice a lot of good, but it's difficult to say why or how. It's just a collection of easy syllables, noises and intervals that focus your voice to a great sound.

YOUR GOALS

GOAL 1
To train your ear so you can sing accurately, 'cos if you can't sing in tune you've got nothing.

GOAL 2
To put an 'edge' on the mid-range where dudes' voices tend to be woolly and tuneless.

GOAL 3
To learn to sing rubbish noises as if you're telling a really good joke (it's called acting).

THEORY
This exercise is like a mantra. A mantra is something you say or sing just before you tackle something difficult or scary like a gig, audition or exam.

EXERCISE 1

THE MANTRA

STEP 1
Listen to both tracks – the slow one and the fast one – following it in the score (the printed music).

STEP 2
Sing through the slow version a couple of times until you are dead accurate.

STEP 3
Technique is the collection of practical things you have to do for really wicked singing. Every time you see this accent ^ over a note, pull the stomach in hard – this is critical. Most of the vowel sounds in this are 'closed' sounds, but there are a few 'open' sounds – 'la-la' and 'ka-ka'. You must push the jaw right down on these 'open' sounds – or you won't get the brightness or sharpness on any of the 'closed' sounds. If your technique is lazy in one part, you'll pay for it in another part. Push the jaw right down, overdo it, and keep the tongue against the bottom teeth throughout, even on 'Oo-la-la'.

STEP 4
Sing it up to speed with the fast track.

HARMONY

Slim slim bim - a - bim, Slim slim bim - a - bim, Oo - la - la, oo - la - la,

KLASH
Slim slim bim - a - bim, Slim slim bim - a - bim, Oo - la - la, oo - la - la

Oo - la, oo - la, oo - la- la. Tring tring tring tring Tring tring tring tring Oo - la - la, oo - la - la

Oo - la, Oo la, Oo - la - la. Tring tring tring tring Tring tring tring tring Oo - la - la, oo - la - la

Oo - la, Oo la, Oo - la - la. Trim trim trim - a - bim, Trim trim trim - a - bim, Trim - a - bim Trim - a - bim.

Oo - la, Oo la, Oo - la - la. Trim trim trim - a - bim, Trim trim trim - a - bim, Trim - a - bim Trim - a - bim.

Trim - a - trim - a - trim - a - bim. Ka ka ka ka ka ka ka ka Ka ka ka ka ka ka ka ka

Trim - a - trim - a - trim - a - bim. Ka ka ka ka ka ka ka ka Ka ka ka ka ka ka ka ka

PROBLEM?

Problem? What problem? If Klash can do it, it must be easy. Just get on with it.

Trim - a - bim, Trim - a - bim, Trim - a, trim a trim-a-bim. Ka ka ka ka ka ka ka ka

Trim - a - bim, Trim - a - bim, Trim - a trim - a trim-a-bim. Ka ka ka ka ka ka ka ka

Ka ka ka ka ka ka ka ka Oo - la - la, oo - la - la Oo - la, Oo la, Oo-la - la.

Ka ka ka ka ka ka ka ka Oo - la - la, oo - la - la Oo - la, Oo la, Oo-la - la.

Ka ka ka ka ka ka ka ka ka ka ka ka ka Ka ka ka ka ka ka ka ka ka ka ka ka ka Hoi!

Ka ka ka ka ka ka ka ka ka ka ka ka Ka ka ka ka ka ka ka ka ka ka ka ka ka Hoi!

TIP

Get a good focus on the 'words'. Sing them in the nose.

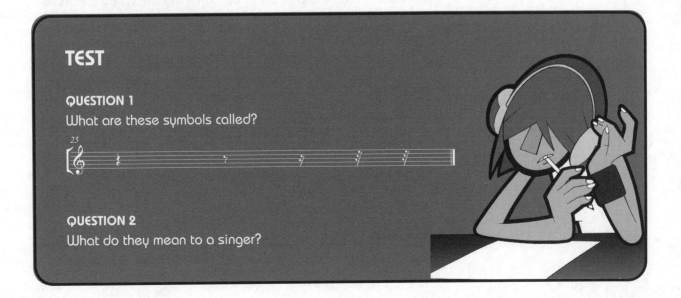

TEST

QUESTION 1

What are these symbols called?

QUESTION 2

What do they mean to a singer?

MAKING A START ON THE LOW NOTES

Low notes might take a bit of practise. A great low sound is called 'resonance'.

YOUR GOALS

GOAL 1
To extend your vocal range downwards.

GOAL 2
To build up some resonance.

THEORY

Low notes are easy, they just take time and patience. You can't force low notes or they go out of tune. Let them grow – it's called 'being organic'. Some work is involved though – it's ok to be organic, and say 'let them grow', but we have got to grow 'em – we need 'technique'.

EXERCISES 1 & 2

BELL-LIKE DEEP NOTES

STEP 1
First listen to Exercise 1 on the track. Stand with both feet firmly on the ground, with your weight equally divided, chest expanded (this is singing in the chest voice), and take a big breath with the stomach.

STEP 2
Put your tongue firmly against your bottom teeth, keep it there throughout, and sing. You should feel it resonate in the nose, the back of the throat and in the chest. It might take a few weeks to build up some practical resonance. Low notes are easy, but they take time and patience.

STEP 3
When you've done Exercise 1 a few times, tackle Exercise 2 in the same way. Do a really good 'Y' sound, chew it up and make a meal of it! This is called 'masticating the note'. You can only really do it on 'Y' sounds, and they focus the voice fantastically.

STEP 4
Try opening up a cavern at the back of your throat in Exercise 2.

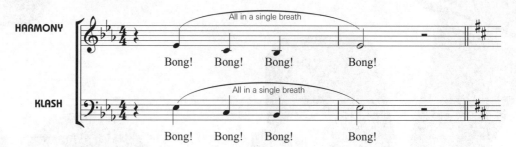

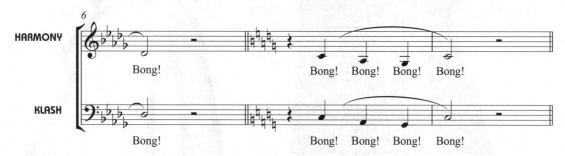

PROBLEM?

If your throat hurts, you are probably letting the tongue wander around aimlessly. Put it forward to the bottom teeth. If your throat still hurts, give it a rest.

TIP

Feel the sound in the pit of the stomach as well as in the nose.

EXERCISE 2

TEST

QUESTION 1

Which part of your body takes the biggest breath? There are three answers to this, but they all mean the same thing.

STARTING ON THE SCREAMS

This is where it starts to get good. Screaming is the most natural sound in the world. We're all born screaming; but we stop it when we learn to be polite and civilised. Well, you don't have to be polite or civilised when you're singing, not if you're an Xtremist. Singing is acting; screaming is acting better – you're a different person when you're screaming. Screaming changes the whole voice – it makes it sound really wicked – and it feels fantastic.

Screaming is the loudest sound a human being can make. You have to go flat out for it. Don't be afraid of it. If you hold back on it, or if you try to do it quietly, you'll hurt your throat. Who ever heard of quiet screaming? It's ridiculous. It's a contradiction. Screaming quietly is really stupid. Even Klash isn't that stupid. But you need to use all your power techniques to support it – your stomach, bum and legs – that's common sense; you can't let your throat take all the punishment, can you?

YOUR GOALS

GOAL 1
To get the highest, loudest sounds a human can make.

GOAL 2
To get rid of all the inhibitions that stop you from 'letting go'. In drama it's called 'exposing yourself emotionally'.

GOAL 3
To feel fantastic!

THEORY

Screaming stretches the soft palate more than anything else does, so the whole voice is sharper, and more resonant.

 EXERCISE 1

GOING HIGH... HIGHER... SCREAMING

In this exercise you'll need to read all of the steps. We'll tell you which bits are for the dudes and which bits are for the babes.

STEP 1

Put both your feet firmly on the floor; don't stand with your weight on one leg, or with your legs crossed. (Why do singers do that?) Get your jaw and your tongue right down to give yourself plenty of room in your mouth. Take a big breath before you start. Fill your stomach with air, puffing it up like a balloon.

STEP 2

Dudes, start off with a crying sound in your 'natural' voice. Pull your stomach in on the first note.

Babes, you might have to start the crying sound in the 'falsetto' voice. Trust your instinct!

HARMONY SAYS

STEP 3

Dudes, go loud enough to get up to the notes. How high you can go in this voice depends on a lot of things: your age, your mind, and how much work you do with the stomach. When you can't go any higher, not even by going louder, go into the 'falsetto' crying sound. Cry like a baby, dude! This bit doesn't have to be loud – you're not up to the screaming pitch yet.

Us babes are already in the 'falsetto' voice by this time. When you're ready – or when you can't get any higher – SCREAM!

STEP 4

SCREAM! Constipate! Bend your knees, go for a fart – take all the strain with your bum and your legs.

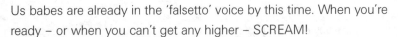

You must use all of your technique for this: jaw, tongue, stomach and constipating.

Us babes should start in the chest voice if you can and go into the head voice as soon as you like.

Start in the natural voice, dudes.

CD TRACK 12

In order to go higher, each phrase must start slightly louder than the previous phrase.

Klash says: Now, dudes, change into a quiet, falsetto whimpering sound.

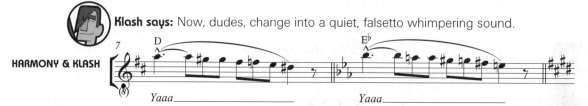

Harmony says: Some of us babes can scream at this pitch. Do it if you can.

Now SCREAM! – constipate!

You may need to slow it down to get full-blooded screams.

This line with 8va means 'sing an octave higher than written'.

TIP

Remember that this is acting – act like a screaming child. Put everything into it. You can't be half-hearted or lazy in this one.

TEST

QUESTION 1

Where should your jaw be in this exercise?

QUESTION 2

Where should you take the strain of the biggest, most outrageous screams?

SMOOTHING DOWN THE VOICE

Smoothing down is very necessary after the screams, but the babes have a different version to the dudes. As always the babes get to go first!

YOUR GOALS

GOAL 1
To start joining up the different voices you have into one coherent voice – 'coherent' means that all parts should make sense with each other.

GOAL 2
To extend the overlap of voices. Traditionally, this is called the 'feigned voice'.

GOAL 3
To reap the benefits of all the different parts of the voice you've been working on: the head voices, the chest voice, the mid-range and the screaming voice.

THEORY (THIS ONE'S FOR THE BABES!)
This is the most important exercise of the lot. It's dead easy. You go from the easy part of the head voice to the easy part of the chest voice.

EXERCISE 1a

THE STACCATO VERSION (SHARP HARMONY)
A staccato dot over a note means that the note is shortened followed by a silence, but the overall timing stays the same. You'll hear how it works on the CD.

STEP 1
The first time you do this exercise, start at Part 2. Sing it quietly, but don't be so quiet that nobody can hear it! Keep your tongue against your bottom teeth throughout this entire exercise. Pull the stomach in gently on the first note of each scale, then let the stomach look after itself.

STEP 2
You will find that there is a change in the voice about half way down the first few scales. Let it change where it wants to!

PART 1

Koo koo koo koo koo koo koo koo   Koo koo koo koo koo koo koo koo

Koo koo koo koo koo koo koo koo   Koo koo koo koo koo koo koo koo

Koo   koo   koo   koo   koo   koo   koo   koo

PART 2

Koo koo koo koo koo koo koo koo   Koo koo koo koo koo koo koo koo

Koo koo koo koo koo koo koo koo   Koo koo koo koo koo koo koo koo

Koo koo koo koo koo koo koo koo   Koo koo koo koo koo koo koo koo

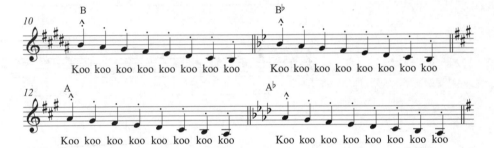

Koo koo koo koo koo koo koo koo   Koo koo koo koo koo koo koo koo

Koo koo koo koo koo koo koo koo   Koo koo koo koo koo koo koo koo

Now we have to change to the bass clef because we're running out of space on the treble clef.

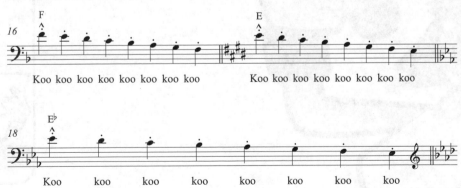

Koo koo koo koo koo koo koo koo   Koo koo koo koo koo koo koo koo

Koo   koo   koo   koo   koo   koo   koo   koo

TIP

In the smooth version, look at your neck in the mirror. Is there a movement on every note? There shouldn't be. If there is, it is because you are jolting from note to note. Slide from note to note so there is no jolting at all – then there won't be any movement in the neck!

EXERCISE 1b

THE SMOOTH VERSION (SMOOTH HARMONY)

STEP 1

Repeat the steps for Exercise 1a, smoothly this time, still keeping it quiet, with your tongue against your bottom teeth. Help the first note with the stomach, and slide over the join between the head voice and chest voice. Start at Part 2

STEP 2.

When you've done all that a few times, and you feel confident with it, start at Part 1.

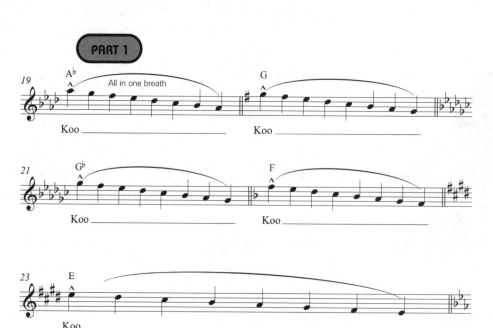

PART 1

19 A♭ All in one breath G Koo Koo

21 G♭ F Koo Koo

23 E Koo

PROBLEM?

Problem? What problem? I told you – it's dead easy – it's supposed to be.

6

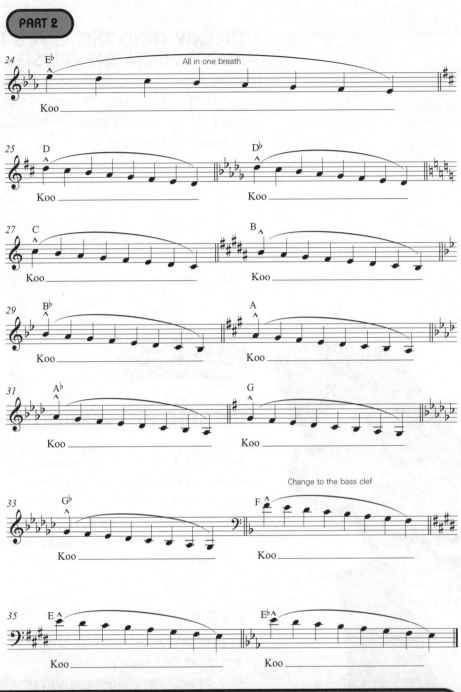

PART 2

TEST

QUESTION 1

To a singer, what does this accent ^ over a note mean? What should you do?

QUESTION 2

What does a dot over a note mean?

QUESTION 3

What does a curved line (a 'slur') ⌒ over or under a group of notes mean? How should you sing them?

CD TRACK 19

THEORY (AND THIS ONE'S TO SEPARATE THE DUDES FROM THE BOYS!)

Dudes, this is the start of a very long sequence that takes years to make perfect – but you can also get some wicked benefits straight away! You have to do this over and over again. Practise it a lot! Downward scales are always good for tone.

EXERCISE 2a

THE STACCATO VERSION (SHARP KLASH)

This is for the dudes. It might look the same as Harmony's version, but it's does different things in dudes' voices. A staccato dot over or under a note means the note is short with a short silence after it, but the overall timing stays the same. You'll hear how it works on the CD. This may be easy for the babes (Harmony hates being called that!), but it's well hard for us dudes!

STEP 1

Put your tongue against your bottom teeth and keep it there throughout this exercise, even when you're breathing. Keep your head down. Take a big breath with the stomach. Pull the stomach in as you sing the first note. For the remaining seven notes let the stomach look after itself. Go quite loud, or the first note will be dodgy. Do each scale in one breath. If you run out of breath before you get to the end, squeeze the stomach to get the last drop of air out.

STEP 2

From bar 4 onwards you have to change voices on either A flat (sometimes called G sharp) or G – all scales contain one or the other. Pull the stomach in on the 'change' note then relax it. So, on some scales, you might have to use the stomach three times.

Now we have to change to the bass clef because we're running out of space on the treble clef.

PROBLEM?

If you really can't get up to the top note on either of these versions, start on the E flat (bars 3 and 19) – everyone can get that E flat in falsetto. If you can't change on the A flat, change on the G or F sharp. Don't change lower than F natural, or it won't lead on to anything better.

EXERCISE 2b

THE SMOOTH VERSION (SMOOTH KLASH)

STEP 1

Go back up to the top and do it all over again smoothly. Basic rules again: tongue against bottom teeth, head down, big breath with the stomach, help the first note and the 'change' note with the stomach and, if you run out of breath, squeeze the stomach to find the extra breath.

PROBLEM?

When you come to change from one voice to another (it's difficult!), try not to go silent between the voices. You're supposed to join them up – not break them up – and try to avoid the unwanted extra low note at the change.

Don't worry if you can't do all of it right at the first attempt. This is difficult, it takes time – do as much of it as you can.

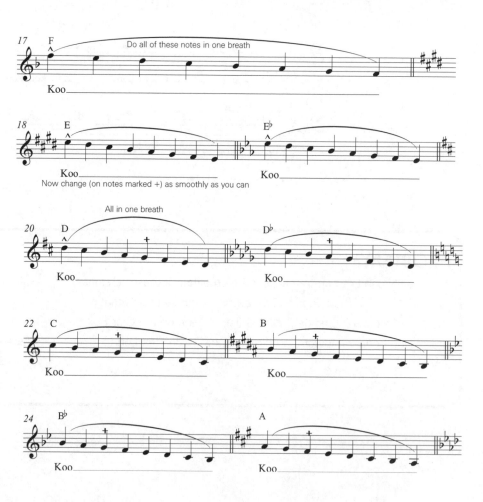

Now try to do it all in the natural voice; if you can't, continue to change on the third note.

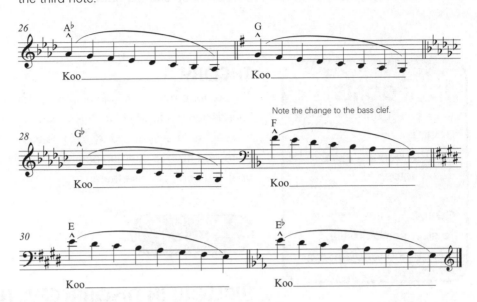

Note the change to the bass clef.

TIP

You need to develop an awareness of how loud to make each note to get the best out of it – ie the best control. This is especially true of the first note and the 'change' note.

TEST

QUESTION 4

For singing dudes, what does this accent ^ mean when it's over a note? What should you do?

QUESTION 5

Why do you think it's missing from bars 21–25? Come on, dudes, you can work this out.

QUESTION 6

What does a dot over a note mean?

QUESTION 7

For a singer, what does a curved line (a 'slur') over a group of notes mean? How should you sing them?

LESSON 6

CD TRACK 23

A BIT OF DEATH METAL

This is the easiest way of getting the loud deep sounds going.

YOUR GOALS

GOAL 1
To extend the range downwards.

GOAL 2
To start some growls, grunge and dirty singing.

THEORY

This exercise makes use of your crying sounds, probably the first sounds you made when you were born. It's acting. Low notes are easy, so keep them easy. If you try to force them you just can't get down there. You have to open up and act. But they take time. Low notes dry up if you don't practise them.

EXERCISE 1

WALLOW IN DISGRACEFUL NOISES

STEP 1

Push the tongue against the bottom teeth. Take in a big breath with the stomach.

STEP 2

Start with a good 'Y', use it to push the jaw right down with the tongue. Make the sounds in your nose, that will make it much louder with no extra effort. It's acting – be a cry baby! Make some disgusting sounds – you know you want to! If you run out of breath, squeeze the stomach to get at those last drops of air.

PROBLEM?

The problem here is obvious. This exercise covers two octaves, and the bottom half could be well hard to get at, even though the notes themselves are quite easy to do. It takes time…! Keep practising, and it will eventually go right down deep. Keep pushing your jaw down with your tongue and, in this position, try to sing the lowest notes through your nose. You'll be surprised how important your nose is for singing. You might get a tickle in your throat. Just keep pushing that jaw down. If your throat hurts – stop. Try again tomorrow.

Don't rush it, give yourself time to make a good crying sound on every note.

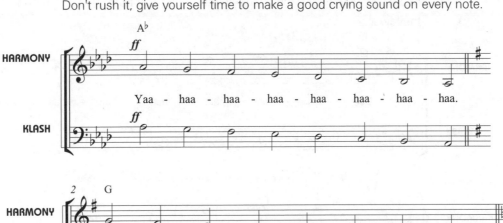

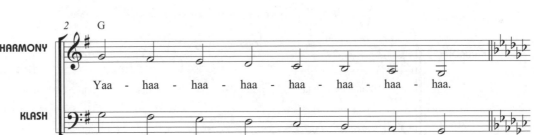

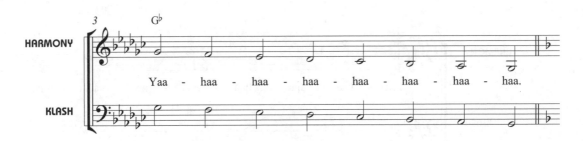

Make sure you get a good crying sound on the first note. That will set up the lower sounds.

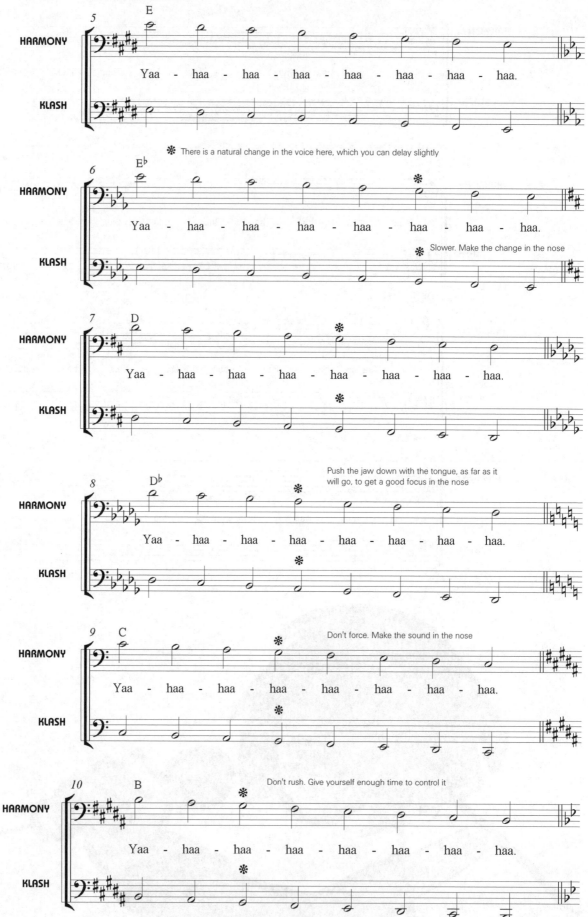

The first note is still crucial.

Now do the whole exercise again

TEST

QUESTION 1

Where should you focus the voice?

CO-ORDINATING THE STOMACH MUSCLES WITH THE VOICE

This is very hard work, but the younger you are the easier it will be to learn. It'll make your voice sound really wicked, and it will give you a lot of control over your tone.

TRACK 25

YOUR GOALS

GOAL 1
To build up the habit of working every note from the stomach.

GOAL 2
To make the whole voice sound dead serious.

GOAL 3
To make singing easier.

THEORY

Now, I know you still think that all singing really comes from the throat, but it doesn't! It's easier, and sounds better, if you do it all from the stomach. You have to learn to do all the work miles away from the throat – even controlling the tone – and the stomach is the best place to do it. It's a lot stronger than the throat. But the stomach is lazy! You have to MAKE it work. You have to learn to co-ordinate the voice with the stomach.

EXERCISE 1

SINGING FROM THE STOMACH

STEP 1
Take a big breath.

STEP 2
Start by singing a long, fairly deep note. It doesn't have to be loud, just loud enough to get a decent focus. If you can't get a good note down there, settle for the best sound you can get; just make sure it's in tune.

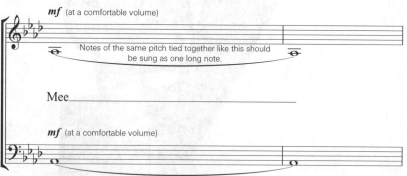

Notes of the same pitch tied together like this should be sung as one long note.

STEP 3

Now repeat it, introducing four loud bits of emphasis by using the stomach (this is also the best and safest way of doing vibrato). Start your long note by pulling in the stomach sharply, making it loud for a split second, then relax, letting the voice continue more quietly. Then repeat it immediately.

TRACK 26 CD

STEP 4

There should be no silences. The note should be continuous, but with a rhythmic pulse. Pull the stomach in on this accent ^.

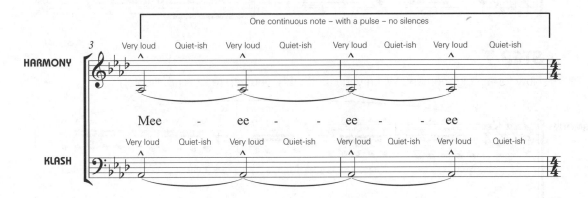

STEP 5

Now try it in a more organised format. There should still be no silences within the phrases.

TRACK 27 CD

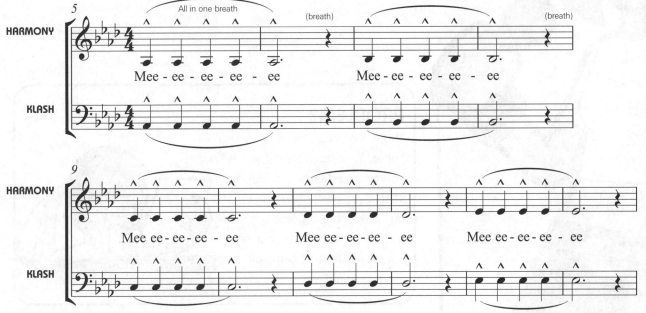

STEP 6

Now let's change the lyric and double the speed. It should sound like a very controlled pulse.

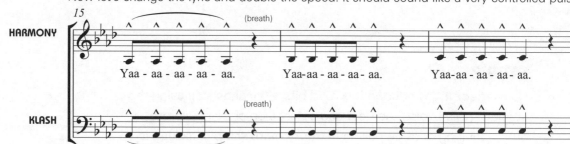

STEP 7

Now for the big moment. When you can do this, you can really sing. Hoorah!

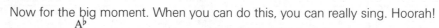

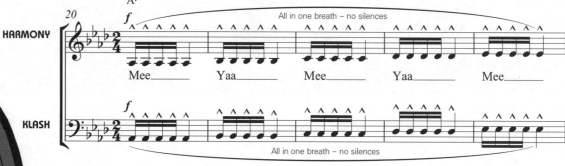

PROBLEM?

This is a problem for all of us babes. Your stomach will be getting tired. Maybe it's 'locking' so that you can't move it in or out. Give it a rest. Come back and do it again later. You don't necessarily have to complete this lesson today.

STEP 8

Now try it going down.

STEP 9

Now try it a little bit higher.

TIP

If your throat hurts but your stomach doesn't – you're not doing enough with your stomach!

TEST

QUESTION 1

When two notes at the same pitch are tied together, how should you sing them?

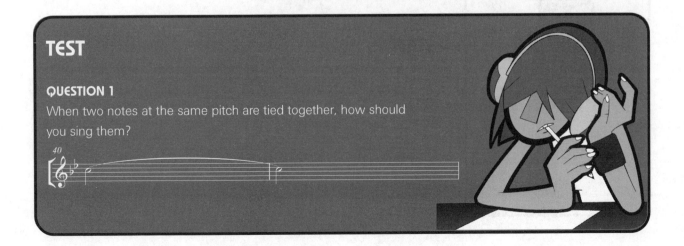

SMOOTHING IT DOWN QUIETLY

There are two exercises in this lesson: one for the dudes, and one for the babes. That's because male and female voices are different. That's called 'stating the rocking obvious'.

YOUR GOALS

GOAL 1
To make the join between the head and chest voices real smooth.

GOAL 2
To start up the mixed voice – it's a wicked sound, like Gold-Metal music.

PROBLEM?
Although it's quiet, it should still be audible. Even the quietest sounds are supposed to be heard!

THEORY
The join between the two voices is called the 'passaggio', well that's what my teacher calls it. The two voices overlap quite a bit – it's called the 'feigned' voice – and, if you can really mix them so that it turns into a sort of blended voice, you can get some dead-good sounds. Mixed voices have to be practised quietly – even by Xtremists!

EXERCISE 1 (FOR THE DUDES!)

MIXED VOICE KLASH

STEP 1
Start with some of the earlier exercises, particularly from Lesson 5, before you do this exercise.

STEP 2
Do all of it quietly. It's easy – it's supposed to be. The only difficult bit is changing from one voice to the other. Start each scale in falsetto, finish in the mixed voice (that means the quiet natural voice) and change where you like!

STEP 3
Do the last two scales totally in the mixed voice. Then go back and do it all again. Over and over…and over…and over…and over…

Start in falsetto, finish quietly in the natural or mixed voice.

It's all very easy, except for the change-note. Try to make the change so smooth that it sounds like one continuous voice.

Keep your tongue against your bottom teeth. If it hurts, you are doing too much. Keep it gentle, but focussed. Watch the tuning.

Do the last two scales entirely in the 'mixed voice' – quietly.

TIP

Dynamics – that means loudness and quietness. In any phrase, the highest note is nearly always supposed to be the loudest. In this exercise it is the first note. So make sure you don't start each scale so quietly that you leave yourself with nowhere to go, or you'll get a big jolt when you change voices – very unconvincing!

TEST

QUESTION 1
What should you do when you're running out of breath and you're not allowed to take a new breath?

PROBLEM?

Watch that your jaw doesn't go up and down with the note – it's your stomach that's supposed to move not your jaw. Only move the jaw on 'yaa', not on the four notes of 'mee'.

EXERCISE 2 (FOR THE BABES!)

MIXED VOICE HARMONY

STEP 1

Before you do this, do some of the earlier exercises in this book, particularly from Lesson 5.

STEP 2

Take a big breath with the stomach, puffing it up a bit. Then pull the stomach in gently for the notes marked ^, and let the stomach out for all the other notes. All the notes in this are easy (you have to look after the easy part as well as the difficult bits). Just let the voice change where it wants to.

STEP 3

'Port.' is short for 'portamento', which, musically, means 'slide'. So slide from note to note. There must be no gaps, jolts or silences between the notes. Keep it dead smooth and quiet!

TIP

This is a good exercise to work on if your voice feels a bit ropey.

TEST

QUESTION 2

Where should your tongue be in all this? Yes, I know it should be in your mouth – I didn't think it would be under your arm! Where, in your mouth, should you put it?

VIBRATO

The mysteries of vibrato are endless. Here, we can only scrape the surface...

YOUR GOALS

GOAL 1
To make a good sound.

GOAL 2
To make a fast shake in the voice that makes the voice sound smoother – a shake that's so good that no one notices it.

GOAL 3
To avoid 'squawkyness'.

GOAL 4
To avoid the 'knock' – that slow, heavy pulsating which seems to interrupt the voice – and drives everyone mad!

THEORY

Vibrato is best done from the stomach, not from the throat or jaw. When you develop a great sound, when your technique is good and your resonance is really wicked, you might notice that your bottom lip is trembling on your best notes. This is the beginning of natural vibrato. Don't force it, don't discourage it, just let it develop naturally while continuing to build up controlled vibrato from the stomach.

EXERCISE 1

INTRODUCING VIBRATO SLOWLY

STEP 1

Now, guys, start this slowly. Take a big breath from the stomach, and start singing loudly – but don't force it. Hold the first note and then introduce a slow, regular pulse from the stomach (on notes marked ^) – a slow vibrato. Keep your head down, and try to keep a hard edge on the tone – the stomach muscles work better with a good sound. It's dead hard to do this with a woolly sound. If you can't get a good sound – go louder!

This wavy line above a note means 'shake the note'. Don't worry if you can't

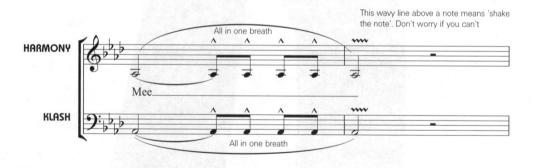

Now try it a tone higher, and with a different syllable.

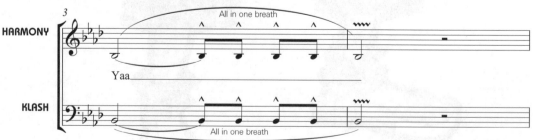

STEP 2

Now, double the speed of the vibrato. That means double the number of stomach pulses, but keep the timing of all the other notes the same.

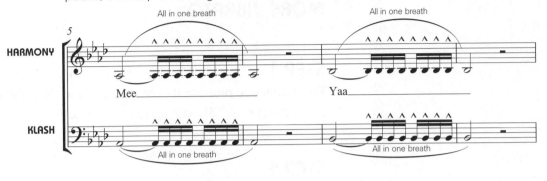

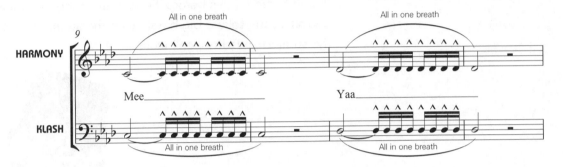

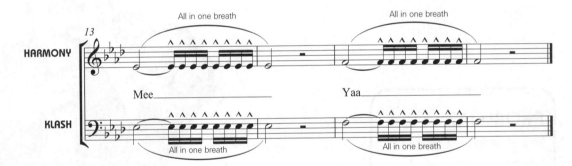

PROBLEM?

This is hard work; but once you've got the knack of it you never lose it.

EXERCISE 2

MORE VIBRATO

STEP 1

Every time you practise this next part, try to do it three times:
(1) fast (2) slow (3) back up to speed again.

STEP 2

You've heard all this before: head down, tongue against your bottom teeth, take a big breath with the stomach, and go loud or the stomach muscles won't work.

PROBLEM?

Your stomach will 'lock' until you get the hang of it all.

CD
TRACKS 39 & 40

Mee_____ yaa_____

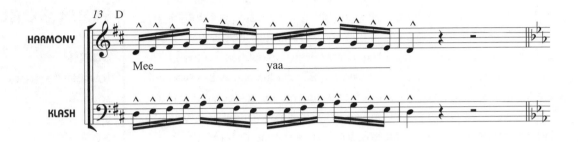

Mee_____ yaa_____

Mee_____ yaa_____

TIP

Keep practising. This technique will never let you down.

TEST

QUESTION 1

If your throat hurts but your stomach doesn't, what does it mean?

XTREME FINALE

It's time to put it all together in spoilt-brat sounds.

THEORY

Going flat out for it, pushing the boat out, letting go, sky-rocketing, and all the other metaphors for throwing inhibitions away, are good for the psychology of becoming a whole human being. All art, including performing on stage, is a child-like activity (Hey, look at us!), so the logical conclusion is to act as a spoilt brat. But, dudes and babes, you are 'cultivated' spoilt brats – you've got the technique to back it up. You have to act – you have to look and sound as if it's all natural. But we know that most performers are shy. We just keep that a secret! That's why most rockers don't really tell the truth in interviews – they keep up the act. So act now!

YOUR GOALS

GOAL 1
To make fantastic rock sounds.

GOAL 2
To have technique so good you can just forget about it.

GOAL 3
To have shocking Xtremes.

SPOILT-BRAT SOUNDS

STEP 1
Put both feet firmly on the floor, with your weight evenly distributed. Dudes, sing the first phrase in the natural voice, if you can. If you can't, take it into the falsetto voice, and then back into the natural voice. Make it sound like crying. If it sounds like 'proper singing' you're not acting it right.

Babes, you should do it in the head voice, but act! Make it a bit screechy!

STEP 2
Pull the stomach in for the top notes, guys and dudes. When it gets up high, constipate – really put your bum into it and go for a fart to get those wicked sounds. Never mind about posture (you're not doing classical singing!), go for the far-out rocky technique that we've been teaching you in these ten lessons. If you're doing it right you'll go dizzy.

STEP 3
Always follow this lesson with smoothing-down exercises from Lessons 5 and 8.

PROBLEM?
The problem is obvious: you're scared of hurting your throat on these outrageous, exposed sounds. If your throat hurts real bad and your stomach and your bum don't – you're not doing enough with your stomach and bum. If it hurts badly – or if your head hurts, which is quite common in these Xtreme exercises – give it a rest. Don't do this exercise too many times in one day. You need to practise, but you're not supposed to be tearing your throat apart. Give it a chance to recover.

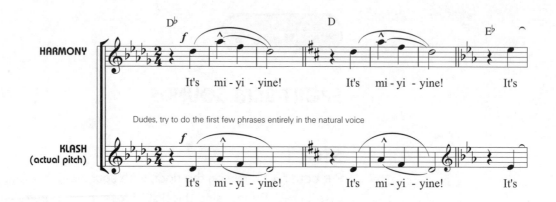

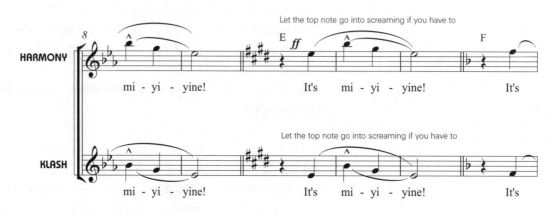

STEP 4

Now go back down, doing the phrases in the reverse order.

TIP

Scream as if you are being tortured!

TEST

QUESTION 1

What part of you should be taking the greatest strain?

TOP 10 ARTISTS

JON BON JOVI

Jon Bon Jovi, who gave his slightly altered name to his band, BON JOVI, is noted for great singing, excellent technique, a big range, and a gravel-edged voice production which takes hard work to produce.

STATISTICS

DATE OF BIRTH
2 March 1962

PLACE OF BIRTH
Perth Amboy, New Jersey

BIRTH NAME
Jon Francis Bongiovi Jr

FIRST SUCCESS
'Runaway' – 1984

TRUE STORY!

One of Bon Jovi's most important albums – *Blaze Of Glory* (1990) – was intended as the soundtrack of the film, *Young Guns II*, although few of the tracks made it into the film.

IN THE STYLE OF...

Jon Bon Jovi has superb technique, combined with an instinct for vocal sound. He knows what sound he wants, what tessitura (area of the vocal range) he needs to sing in, and what technique is required to produce it. The gravel in the voice is a mixture of acting and huge muscular support from the waist down; it is hard work, and he doesn't always dirty the sound in live gigs. His singing is characterised by tremendous tension in the sounds, provided by tension in the stomach and leg muscles, so his singing never sounds trivial. All BON JOVI songs are good voice-builders in their original versions. This is often a feature of great rock singers: their songs tend to be exceptionally good vocal exercises in a way that pop songs are not.

Songs from *Slippery When Wet* and *Blaze of Glory* display the fully-matured Jon Bon Jovi technique: the jaw and the tongue right down to enable the big range, the full force of the personality and flexible tone control; the hard work of the stomach muscles, giving a dark, even sinister, side to the music; and the gravel in the voice manufactured from the stomach.

LISTEN TO
'Livin' On A Prayer'
'Blood Money'
'Santa Fe'

SKIN

STATISTICS

DATE OF BIRTH
3 August 1967

PLACE OF BIRTH
London, England

BIRTH NAME
Deborah Anne Dyer

FIRST SUCCESS (WITH SKUNK ANANSIE)
'Little Baby Swastika'

Skin from Skunk Anasie is a rarity – a really successful female hard-rock singer. There are plenty of women who are good hard-rock singers; but they tend not to be successful because the odds are stacked against women in the rock world. Male rockers regard the admittance of women rockers as revolutionary.

TRUE STORY!

Before her success as a singer, Skin studied interior design and – according to legend – earned her living as a bouncer in a London club.

IN THE STYLE OF...

LISTEN TO

'Brazen (Weep)'
'All I Want'

Skin has a huge range, excellent technique, and a need to show off every part of the voice: a need that every singer should have.

Most of 'All I Want' is well within the compass of inexperienced rock singers, and it paves the way for something more demanding. Skin starts with a standard yell: 'yeah yo!' on the E, mostly in chest voice, but it's coloured with some head voice and supported strongly by the diaphragm and other power muscles below the waist. This is to get the voice started, the jaw and tongue down, and the technique up and running. Always do the extra notes, vowels and yells that great singers do; they're nearly always vocal exercises (sometimes unwitting) – a singer of Skin's calibre knows exactly what she is doing. The verses should then present you with few problems; the song is predominantly at the top of the chest voice, where the power is immense. You will need to constipate on phrases like 'burn away'. It is also a good idea to do some screaming exercises. Do the falsetto squeaks, such as on 'want…want' at the end of the chorus. This song is hard work – you cannot be lazy in a Skunk Anansie number.

SEBASTIAN BACH

If ever a singer had everything, that singer is Sebastian Bach of Skid Row: looks, talent, the most beautiful voice in rock history, tall athletic physique, physical strength, an unrivalled instinct for tone quality, the gift of the gab, an endless capacity for driving himself on – and (rumour has it) he was born rich.

TRUE STORY!

Sebastian Bach did a season on Broadway in the stage musical of *Dr Jekyl And Mr Hyde*, playing the dual leading role. He has now embarked on a solo career with albums and tours.

STATISTICS

DATE OF BIRTH
3 April 1968

PLACE OF BIRTH
Freeport, Bahamas

BIRTH NAME
Sebastian Bierk

FIRST SUCCESS
Skid Row – 1989

IN THE STYLE OF...

LISTEN TO
'18 And Life'
' I Remember You'

This is a singer who wants to be able to do everything: the perfect mixed voice – not just a mix of natural voice and falsetto, but he's taken it a stage further and incorporated screaming into the mix – and also opened up a huge chest voice. He's built up a huge range.

There is no such thing as an easy Skid Row number, but '18 And Life' is about the easiest. The predominant note in this is top A flat. Do whatever you have to do to get those notes. If you cannot get the line 'fingers to the bone', scream them: they are top D flats. You need to constipate like mad in this song; but it will be worth it. Every time you come to a phrase you cannot do – scream it. Sooner or later it will all join up, and your voice will be better than it was on everything else.

WHITNEY HOUSTON

STATISTICS

DATE OF BIRTH
9 August 1963

PLACE OF BIRTH
Newark, New Jersey

BIRTH NAME
Whitney Houston

FIRST SUCCESS
'Saving All My Love For You'
– 1986

Whitney Houston's mother is the celebrated gospel singer, Cissy Housten, and Whitney learned her craft singing in a gospel choir from the age of eleven.

SUPERSTAR TIP

In each phrase or line – no matter what the overall pitch – pick out the highest note and squeeze the stomach on that one note. You'll be surprised at the improvement in your rapport with the audience.

IN THE STYLE OF...

LISTEN TO

'The Greatest Love Of All'
'I Will Always Love You'
'Saving All My Love For You'

Whitney Houston is not generally thought of as an Xtremist (too emotionally detached, for one thing), but she is technically brilliant, and her songs are generally well-crafted and good voice-builders. There is a pronounced R&B influence in her singing, which is highly accomplished, even technically brilliant.

In 'The Greatest Love Of All', each verse starts gently and builds up the voice and technique to a big climax at the end of the chorus. Start with a big breath, use all of your technique in the verse – jaw and tongue down on the open sounds, pull the stomach in every time the tune goes up, let it out when it goes down. In the chorus, for the big notes – constipate: particularly on 'if I fail, if I succeed…' and the final 'the greatest love of all is easy to achieve'.

You will need a lot of breath control for this song. The lines are long and sustained so take big breaths with the stomach and, when the breath begins to run out, squeeze the stomach so that you squeeze the last ounce of breath out.

PAUL MCCARTNEY

Paul McCartney was the most accomplished singer of The Beatles, stretching his range more than was generally thought possible for a man in the '60s. In 'Oh Darling' he was sustaining top Ds in a good mixed voice; this is higher than most operatic tenors could sing. He is a good example of a singer whose voice has continued to improve because he continually stretched it.

STATISTICS

DATE OF BIRTH
18 June 1942

PLACE OF BIRTH
Liverpool, England

BIRTH NAME
James Paul McCartney

FIRST SUCCESS
'Love Me Do' – 1962

SUPERSTAR TIP

Write a song every day. Get somebody else to give you a subject and no matter how daft (like 'Penny Lane'?) write a song with that title.

IN THE STYLE OF...

Paul McCartney, with his instinct for sounds, his inventiveness, and his determination, was always going to be a leading light of The Beatles. It showed in his need to do everything better than everyone else. In his singing he had to go higher than anyone else, while keeping a casual sound; effectively, this meant that he developed the mixed head voice further than anyone at that time. The results were wonderful, and are continuing. Whether he knew what he was doing is a moot point.

The crucial thing is to treat it all as the male mixed-head voice. Keep it 'natural' – try to make it sound as if you've never had a singing lesson. You have to develop an instinct for how loud to go for each note. Too quiet, and you won't get the high notes; too loud, and you'll blow yourself off the note altogether. Support all the high notes from the stomach, and constipate like mad.

LISTEN TO
'Love Me Do'
'Eleanor Rigby'
'Oh, Darling'
'Ebony And Ivory'

SKYE

STATISTICS

DATE OF BIRTH
25 May 1972

PLACE OF BIRTH
London, England

BIRTH NAME
Shirley Kleris Yionavieve Edwards

FIRST SUCCESS
Who Can You Trust? – 1996

Skye is one of the world's best pop/rock singers, noted for her extraordinarily beautiful tone and wide range. Her live singing benefits from a considerable acting ability and stagecraft: more than most singers, she 'knows what it should look like'. She was the lead singer of MORCHEEBA for eight years, and is now pursuing a solo career.

TRUE STORY!

Skye's favourite numbers from her time spent singing with Morcheeba are 'Rome Wasn't Built In A Day' and 'Blindfold'.

IN THE STYLE OF...

LISTEN TO
'Blindfold'
'Rome Wasn't Built In A Day'

Skye's technique is excellent. She has stretched her range (you can hear how much on the Exercise CDs which accompany *The Complete Vocal Workout* [Sanctuary]. This has enabled her to produce wonderful tone quality.

'Blindfold' is a simple song with no difficult notes; so why can you not make it sound right? Why does it sound feeble when you try it? Why do some notes not 'click in', and others crack or yodel? The answer is that you need to exercise the full range to have control over the notes in the middle of the voice. Bear in mind that Morcheeba is not a loud band. Their gigs are quite comfortable on the ear, so it would be inappropriate for the singer to go flat-out as if she were in a heavy metal band; but she needs to exercise the same range as a heavy metal singer.

BONO

The story is that his strange stage name is derived from a teenage nickname, 'Bono Vox', which is joke-Latin for 'good voice'. There was a shop in Dublin which sold 'Bonovox' hearing aids – maybe this prompted the name.

SUPERSTAR TIP!

U2 considered replacing Bono as they thought his voice did not come up to scratch. He certainly proved them wrong – ignore what others think and concentrate on what you want to do.

STATISTICS

DATE OF BIRTH
10 May 1960

PLACE OF BIRTH
Balleymun, Dublin, Ireland

BIRTH NAME
Paul David Hewson

FIRST SUCCESS
U2 Three (EP) – 1979

IN THE STYLE OF...

Of all the singers around at the moment, Bono is the one who most male singers want to emulate: those bright, exciting, fruity sustained high notes; that wonderful 'bite' in the low lines; the spin he puts on the words (which are always very clear). He seems able to sing absolutely anything – who wouldn't want to do all that?

In the first half of 'With Or Without You', go for a hard edge. This is very important – don't let these notes be woolly or feeble. You may need to sing louder than he does to focus them in the nose. They are not particularly low, but they are definitely in the chest voice, and they must have bite. On that first high line, 'With or without you', take a huge breath with the diaphragm (you have plenty of time to do it) and pull the diaphragm in for the high notes. The big leaps in this song are difficult; you need to go loud on the high notes to manage the shift. For the 'Wow! Wow! Wow!' you need a quick big breath from the stomach – not with the throat or you'll blow yourself off the note – and constipate. Do that wonderful last quiet falsetto phrase – it's a great exercise.

LISTEN TO

'With Or Without You'
'Pride'
'I Still Haven't Found What I'm Looking For'

ELLA FITZGERALD

STATISTICS

DATE OF BIRTH
25 April 1918

PLACE OF BIRTH
Newport News, Vancouver

BIRTH NAME
Ella Fitzgerald

FIRST SUCCESS
'A Tisket, A Tasket' – 1938

The divine Ella Fitzgerald – she may belong to a different age, but the singing is fantastic and technically brilliant.

TRUE STORY!
By the '50s Ella Fitzgerald was the most famous non-classical female singer in the world. She was still able to fill theatres in the '90s.

IN THE STYLE OF...

LISTEN TO
'You Do Something To Me'
'Love Me Or Leave Me'

Ella worked from the diaphragm, breathed deeply with it, kept pushing her jaw down (which always made it look as if she was having a wonderful time), and kept her tongue flat and against her bottom teeth. There was a voluptuousness about her singing. Try to see the Bing Crosby television shows of the '50s – she was a frequent guest and you can see the technique in full throttle.

It's good to work on a song with such well-crafted lyrics as 'You Do Something To Me'. Start with a big breath and sing that glorious, slow first line. Do not shy away from the 'oo' sounds; don't turn the first two words into 'Yoe doe', or you will get none of the glorious sound. You will also lose that magnificently silly display of assonance 'Do do that voodoo that you do so well'. Keep taking big breaths and, when you come to the higher notes of 'Let me live 'neath your spell', on the word 'me' squeeze the stomach with all the breath inside it.

JAMES WALSH

James Walsh is the lead singer of STARSAILOR. He is undoubtedly talented. Watch the jaw come right down on the long-sustained phrases, while he keeps the tongue flat.

SUPERSTAR TIP

Concentrate on your technique. Don't be afraid to drop your jaw if you need a little more room. Sing loud enough to get a beautiful smiling sound. Never force it, and keep the tongue flat.

STATISTICS

DATE OF BIRTH
9 June 1978

PLACE OF BIRTH
Chorley, England

BIRTH NAME
James Walsh

FIRST SUCCESS
'Fever' – 2001

IN THE STYLE OF...

LISTEN TO
'Poor Misguided Fool'
'Silence Is Easy'

Here is a superb singer who has yet to find his feet (that's probably true of all good singers). Watch his jaw and his tongue and notice how he incorporates his technique into that smile. There is the feeling among some inexperienced singers that such technique will look unnatural and make the words difficult to sing; but James is proof that it produces great results and looks totally natural. He specialises in sustained quiet singing in long, fairly high phrases, which is technically difficult.

The scale of sound is larger than usual in 'Silence Is Easy', probably due to the influence of Phil Spector, who co-produced it; but the gentleness remains the same. This requires greater concentration and more support. This is tiring on the throat muscles, so your throat is likely to feel exhausted, but not sore.

GEORGE MICHAEL

STATISTICS

DATE OF BIRTH
25 June 1963

PLACE OF BIRTH
Bushey, England

BIRTH NAME
Yorgos Kyriatou Panayioutou

FIRST SUCCESS
'Wham Rap!' – 1982

George Michael's remarkable voice is characterised by exceptional beauty of tone, a wide range, and very little vibrato. Most singers can't get away with a straight note, it is usually painful to listen to; but George does not seem to need vibrato to make his voice interesting.

SUPERSTAR TIP

Sing from your hips, really act with them, they should ache if you're doing it right. Find the best position for your head on every note and incorporate it into your act.

IN THE STYLE OF...

LISTEN TO

'Wake Me Up Before You Go Go'
'Master And Servant'
'Faith'

Don't underestimate the importance of his time with Wham! It was crucial to the development of his voice and his technique. You need to watch the videos to see the physical technique, to see how he incorporates the positions of his head, the movement of his hips and posterior. The great thing about George is that he was never coy in singing with his whole body.

Although George was miming, as is the convention of pop videos, in 'Wake Me Up Before You Go Go', he unwittingly mimed the singing technique. It's very difficult not to do that, once you have made the technique second nature. Keep pushing the jaw down on the open sounds.

The full glory of George's wonderful phrasing blossoms in 'Faith'. Again, look at the video and watch the head movements: he appears to be emoting, but every head position is designed to achieve a specific sound. Watch the jaw and tongue going right down, giving him plenty of space in the mouth. Listen for the precise use of vibrato; he seems to be able to produce beautiful sounds without much vibrato.

NOTES

NOTES

GLOSSARY

ABSOLUTE PITCH

This is also called 'perfect pitch'. This means you can always sing the right note whatever's going on, even if the band is all wrong. Hardly anyone's pitch is absolute or perfect. (See 'relative pitch'.)

ADAM'S APPLE

The lump on the front of a dude's neck. This is the thyroid cartilage, part of the larynx. Although it can move a bit, don't touch it. Babes have a similar structure, but smaller, so it doesn't stick out like an Adam's apple.

ACCENTS

These are symbols in music. They tell you the way certain notes should be sung. Here are a few common ones: ^ means marcato, or heavily marked, always pull the stomach in on this one; > means accentuate, make it stand out from the other notes; - means tenuto, or hold the note slightly longer than the other notes, but not so long as a pause.

ALLEGRO

This is an Italian word meaning 'fast'.

CAPPELLA, OR A CAPPELLA

Italian for 'chapel', or in a chapel or church style. It has now come to mean 'unaccompanied singing'.

CAROTIDS, OR CAROTID ARTERIES

There are two of these on each side of your neck: one on the inside and one on the outside. They are your main suppliers of blood to your head. You can see the outside carotid arteries when you don't breath properly; they look like pipes on the side of your neck. This is probably where the word garrotte ('strangle') comes from; so be careful!

THE DIAPHRAGM

This is a muscle, it's the floor of the lungs, it's often called the 'dome-shaped muscle', but, really, it spends a lot of time more or less flat. For centuries the diaphragm was thought to provide support and manipulation for the voice, and that when you pulled in the stomach for high notes, you were pulling in the diaphragm. We now know that the diaphragm moves very little during singing. When singers talk about the diaphragm, what they really mean is the front abdominal muscles, which are right across the front of the stomach, roughly around the naval. This is the bit of you that really moves when you think you are working the diaphragm. But singers and singing teachers continue to refer to the front abdominal muscles as the diaphragm – it's a convenient word, and singing teachers know what it means. (See also 'the stomach muscles'.)

DOMINANT

The fifth note of any diatonic scale and the chord built on it.

F

Forte (pronounced for-tay). An Italian word meaning 'loud' or 'strong'.

FF

Fortissimo. Italian for 'very loud'.

FALSETTO

For babes this is the head voice. For dudes it's the childish crying sound that we can all do from the day we're born to the day we die. But for everyone it's the healing part of the voice. No matter what state your voice is in, if you can get the falsetto voice working, you will find the rest of your voice will also work. Dudes can mix it with the natural headvoice, to magical effect. Babes can mix it with the chestvoice, and that's a fantastic sound. You should exercise your falsetto every day. When you attempt the sounds you want, you trust your ear, in other words you act, and your brain does the computing sub-consciously. It's not the same for babes and dudes. A dude has a natural headvoice and a falsetto headvoice; Babes' headvoice is the same as the falsetto headvoice. Dudes have an extra voice.

FEIGNED VOICE

This is a really old-fashioned term and it's thoroughly confusing. It means the overlap between the head and chest voices. If you combine the voices into a smooth mixed voice you can get a really wicked sound.

FOCUS

This means the hard edge on the sound of the voice; it's sometimes called the metallic edge. You can make it into a really bright sound, like Bono's or Whitney's. What happens is this: You focus your voice on the hard palate, but it feels as if you're singing in your nose. It halves the work of singing. An unfocussed voice has a 'woolly' sound which is easily drowned-out or swamped by the rest of the band. Microphones do not pick up unfocussed voices very well; but even a bad microphone will transmit a well-focussed voice comparatively easily.

GLOTTIS

The space at the upper end of the windpipe between the vocal folds. By opening, closing, widening and narrowing it, the brain modulates it to produce the sound you are thinking of. Leave it alone; your sub-conscious will look after it.

HARD PALATE

The front half of the roof of the mouth, from the top row of teeth and the bony part of the top gum (the real stiff upper lip: dreadful cliché!), to half-way back in the mouth, where it meets the soft palate in a V-shaped join. It's rock hard, and it forms the floor of the nasal sinus, that's the large resonant cavity behind the nose. By focussing the voice on the hard palate you will double the size of your voice in both power and range. Whenever you hear a magical voice, you are listening to hard-palate resonance. It will feel as if you are focussing in the nose. In order to focus on the hard palate you need to stretch the soft palate (see 'soft palate') mostly by singing high notes.

JAW

The only moveable bone in the human head, hinged to the rest of the skull under each ear, roughly speaking. When your jaw drops, your throat opens; but when it is only half-way down it tends to lock, and your throat becomes tight. This will cause you problems, guys, when you try to move from one register to another. You'll find that you can't get up or down to the notes you want; your whole throat will feel as if it's locked. Never be afraid to drop your jaw if you need a little more room. Keeping the jaw down (at least on the open sounds – and that means most sounds) is the single most important technique in singing. (See also 'the tongue'.)

LEGATO

The Italian word for 'smoothly'. A fine legato (a very smooth, well focussed, vocal line) is the most prized ability among professional singers and instrumentalists, from classical to rock. It is really the defining characteristic of the great singer. These are the sounds that really 'send' you. For babes, it is best achieved by smoothing over the join between the head voice and the chest voice, with the mixed voice. For dudes, it requires mastery of the quiet mixed headvoice.

LARYNX

A hollow, muscular organ providing the air passage to the lungs, and holding the vocal chords. It's situated at the front of your neck. It is also known as the 'voice box', which is self-explanatory. The problem is that

we now know that the larynx is not the sole maker of the voice, so although we know that it is important in singing, we don't really know it's function. It obviously regulates something. Never touch the larynx with your fingers, guys. Let the brain sort it out.

MEZZA VOCE, OR MESSA DI VOCE

Italian phrases meaning, 'half voice' or 'mix of the voice'. American singing teachers use these expressions a lot. In practice, both phrases mean singing quietly. It's just another name for the mixed voice, dudes. (See 'mixed voice'.)

MIXED VOICE

This is different for men and women. For dudes, there are basically two mixed voices: the quiet mixed headvoice, in which the falsetto voice is mixed with the natural head voice to produce a smooth magical sound; and the screaming mixed voice, which takes the principle to extremes and mixes screaming with the natural head voice. Mixing the voices is the most difficult of all singing skills. It is also the most important, because it is all about controlling the type of sounds you want. Unlike most singing skills, mixing the voices is not principally about power or range, although both your power and your range will improve from it. When you've worked at both mixed voices, you will eventually be able to mix the two mixed voices. It generally takes about four years. Then you will be able to move smoothly, in a single breath, from a full scream to a delicately modulated magical sound without any jolts or 'gear changes'. This is wicked stuff, dudes.

For babes, the mixed voice is a mixture of head and chest voices. For a long time most singing teachers thought that only dudes could do the mixed voice, but it's now obvious that a lot of babes can do it just as well as the dudes. You've got to do a lot of patient work. It's not actually difficult – all the notes are easy – it just takes

a long time, but the sound is fantastic. It starts in the area of your voice where the chest voice overlaps with the head voice. This used to be called the feigned voice. In time, you can extend it for about two octaves, and then you can join it up smoothly with all the other parts of the voice. Its primary function is to give dynamic control, flexibility and smoothness to an area of the voice where singers are prone to stumble over a lot of 'breaks' and changes.

MODERATO

An Italian word meaning 'at a moderate speed'.

NODULES, OR NODES ON THE VOCAL CHORDS

Few words can make singers panic quite so much as the suggestion that they might get nodules. A nodule is a small swelling or aggregation of cells, even a small tumour. In other words, nodules are usually warts. If you are prone to warts you will get warts. There is not much evidence that they are caused by singing, merely that if you are a singer you are more likely to notice nodules on the vocal chords than if you are, for instance, a bricklayer. Nodules are quite rare. The vast majority of singers never get them, no matter how much they ill-treat the voice. Others get nodules no matter how careful they are. Some singers have had operations to remove nodules but they usually grow back. If you leave them alone they are likely to disappear in a matter of months. If you suspect that you have them, you must seek medical advice.

P

Piano, an Italian word meaning 'quiet' or 'soft'.

PP

Pianissimo, Italian for 'very quiet' or 'doubly soft'.

PASSAGGIO

An Italian word meaning 'passage', which has many uses in music. In singing, it means the point where the voice passes from one register to another. The most important passaggio in the female voice is from the headvoice to the chestvoice. Although it is fixed on A flat in all voices, it can be delayed when approached from either direction, giving the singer the choice of whether to sing a given phrase in chest- or headvoice. The main passaggio in the male voice is from the falsetto headvoice to the natural headvoice. Unlike the female passaggio, this is extremely moveable, and depends largely on how high dudes can go in the natural headvoice. The higher you can go, the more flexible it is. Traditionally, singers are supposed to smooth over the passaggio so that nobody can hear the change; but modern singers often like to accentuate the difference between the voices for dramatic effect. A good singer will be able to do both.

RANGE

This is the distance between your highest and lowest notes; not the distance you can make your voice travel.

RELATIVE PITCH

This is something most of us claim to have. Whereas perfect pitch is the ability to identify and sing any specific note under any circumstances, relative pitch is the ability to identify and sing any specific note in relation to any other note. If I played a note on the keyboard and told you it was an 'A' and asked you to sing an 'E flat' from it, you would be able to do it without hesitation – if you had true relative pitch. There's no connection between relative pitch and absolute pitch, because relative pitch is depend on what you've just heard and absolute pitch doesn't dependent on anything: you either know the note or you don't. Surprisingly, relative pitch is rarer than absolute pitch.

REST

Musically speaking, it's a silence which is part of the music. Although it does not necessarily mean that all the instruments or voices are silent at the same time. A rest is any intentional gap of a specific length of time (as opposed to a pause, which might be unspecific) in any of the vocal or instrumental lines. So when you see it on the page, guys, keep your trap shut: it's someone else's turn.

RIB CAGE

The bony cage around the lungs and other organs; the skeleton of the chest attached to the rest of the skeleton by the vertebrae (backbone). Slightly flexible, it expands when the lungs fill with air. There is evidence that the ribs vibrate with the voice, and possibly act as sound posts. As yet, this is unconfirmed, but I tend to believe it, because singing in the chest voice is such a pleasant sensation.

SCAT

Improvised singing using sounds imitating instruments instead of words. It is usually either fast and spectacular or slow and discordant, the latter involves playing tricks with the pitch by 'bending' the note or using quarter tones. It's an important part of the jazz tradition – Ella Fitzgerald was a great scat singer.

SF OR SFZ

Sforzando, an Italian word meaning 'sudden force' or 'sudden loudness'. You should always produce it by slamming in the stomach muscles, guys. Often the music reverts immediately to a quieter sound.

SIMILE

The Italian word for 'the same' or 'similarly'. It means you should continue singing in the same style (eg legato, staccato, loudly, quietly, etc) as in the previous few bars.

SINUSES

Cavities in the head which resonate with the sounds of the voice. The sinuses are where the tone quality is made. When you have a virus (such as a cold) the sinuses can become clogged and the voice quality becomes difficult to control. Experienced singers can usually clear them out in the normal process of singing, or with vocal exercises if the clogging is not too serious. The quiet mixed headvoice in men, and the quiet headvoice in women, seem to be made almost entirely in the sinuses.

SOFT PALATE

This is the back half of the roof of the mouth; it goes from the V-shaped join with the hard palate, right to the back of the throat. It controls the tone of the entire voice. It's pure muscle, guys, so it needs to be stretched in order to work efficiently, like all muscles. You stretch it by singing your highest notes. Conversely (there's a posh word! it means 'look at it from the other side, guys') you can improve your ability to reach high notes by arching it – try doing that for a difficult high note. This enables you to focus on the hard palate. If you don't stretch the soft palate it acts like a cushion and your notes will sound woolly. Yawning is a very good way of stretching the soft palate.

STACCATO

Italian word meaning 'stopped'. A staccato note is a shortened note followed by a silence, usually represented on the page by a note with a small dot over it. This means that you don't sing the full length of the note, you sing half of it, leaving a silence for the other half of its length. A staccato phrase is a series of short notes separated by silences. It can be very effective for pointing up the words, making them sound 'clipped'.

THE STOMACH MUSCLES

These include the diaphragm and the front abdominal muscles. Singers and singing teachers continue to refer to these muscles collectively as the diaphragm.

You can use the stomach muscles for seven singing techniques.

• Controlling the breath.
• Supporting difficult notes, usually high notes.
• Emphasising certain notes or words, and generally shaping phrases.
• Power.
• Vibrato.
• Tension in phrasing, emoting and tone control.
• Expanding the chest and rib cage.

TECHNIQUE

This means doing it the way we've taught you, not just blasting out from the throat. There are four basic techniques:

• Push the jaw down on the open sounds, particularly on 'I' 'yeah' 'all', 'always'.
• Keep the tongue against the bottom teeth or bottom gum as much as you can. When you have to move it for letters such as L, D, or TH, put it back to the bottom teeth as soon as you can. Watch James Walsh (STARSAILOR); he does it right.
• Those first two techniques open up the throat and stop it from getting damaged.
• When you've got a difficult bit to sing – pull your stomach in or constipate. Always concentrate on your stomach when you're scared of the note.
• Keep your head down – except for special techniques – so keep it down nearly all the time.

TEETH

Very important for singing tone. Try to keep the tip of your tongue against your bottom teeth as much as possible, guys – during both singing and breathing – particularly if you think you are in danger of coughing. False teeth should make no difference; sing with them in exactly the same way, as if they were naturally yours.

TENSION

In singing there is good tension and bad tension. Tension in the neck,

shoulders, or at the base of the tongue is bad. Tension in the actual sound of the voice is good; it arrests the ear and makes people want to listen to you. Tension in the stomach, legs and bum is often good: these are the principal ways of introducing tension into the voice. Experiment with tension in the stomach through whole phrases, particularly in ballads where you might need a better sound on long notes. But keep your shoulders down and relaxed.

THROAT

This is a vague term. Where, for instance, does it begin and end? As far as this book is concerned, by 'throat' we mean the part that is sore when we say we have a sore throat: the inside of the neck. It is the weakest part of the body. It contains a series of regulators, larynx, vocal folds, etc, which are extremely delicate. It is capable of almost no power, it merely regulates and transmits the sound. If you try to force power from the throat, not only is it likely to become sore, but also you'll go out of tune. This is because the regulators, which control your ability to pitch accurately, have become bruised temporarily.

Nearly all of our defence mechanisms are in the throat, it is the chief way into the body; under pressure we tend to 'close the gate', causing soreness, or a lump in the throat. The way to stop it is to drop the jaw and keep the tongue against the bottom teeth. If you can't stop locking the jaw or the throat you might be developing a psychological block; your teacher should be able to help you solve it. In order to do nothing with the throat, you must do everything with the stomach

TONGUE

Klash is right: the tongue is the only muscle in the human body which is stronger in a woman than in a man. Keeping your tongue down to your bottom teeth or gum is crucial; it automatically opens the throat. If you

allow your tongue to wander about aimlessly, your throat will start working overtime, until it runs out of energy. It is better to keep your tongue down and make your stomach do the work.

TONIC

The keynote and the chord built on it.

TRACHEA

Your windpipe; it's the passage which carries the air from the larynx to the bronchial tubes. It's reinforced with cartilage rings.

UVULA

The fleshy extension at the back of the soft palate hanging above the throat. Leave it alone.

VIBRATO

Italian word meaning 'shaking' or 'vibrating'. Singing needs vibrato, particularly on long notes. A totally straight note is not usually attractive – George Michael is an exception. Some natural vibrato is likely to develop in the tiny muscles in and around your jaw and in your lower lip. Neither discourage it nor force it: let it develop of its own accord. If you want to control your vibrato, you should always start it from the stomach. Do not fall into the trap of locking the jaw in order to produce a shake; you will run into all sorts of problems that way, not least, you are likely to look about 80 years old.

VOCAL CHORDS OR VOCAL FOLDS

These are folds in the lining membrane of the larynx, near the glottis. The edges vibrate in the process of singing; it is these vibrations which are thought to make the voice, but that is now in doubt. They are tiny and flat. They are never visible from the outside of the neck. If you think you can see them standing out on your neck, you are probably looking at the carotid arteries.

ANSWERS TO TEST QUESTIONS

LESSON 1 – THE BASICS

1. Getting the jaw down on the open sounds such as: 'ah' or 'aa'.
2. Putting the tongue against the bottom teeth.

LESSON 2 – FOCUSSING IN THE MID-RANGE

1. Rests.
2. Silence. It's someone else's turn, so keep your trap shut.

LESSON 3 – MAKING A START ON THE LOW NOTES

1. Stomach, diaphragm or front abdominal muscles.

LESSON 4 – STARTING ON THE SCREAMS

1. Right down.
2. Your stomach and your bum.

LESSON 5 – SMOOTHING DOWN THE VOICE

1. Pull the stomach in.
2. Keep it short, with a silence after it.
3. Sing all the notes covered by the slur smoothly in a single breath.
4. Pull the stomach in.
5. The accent is missing from bars 21-25 because the 'change' note has become more difficult than the first note.
6. Keep it short with a silence after it.
7. Sing all the notes covered by the slur smoothly without a break, and in a single breath.

LESSON 6 – A BIT OF DEATH METAL

1. In the nose.

LESSON 7 – CO-ORDINATING THE STOMACH MUSCLES WITH THE VOICE

1. As one continuous note.

LESSON 8 – SMOOTHING IT DOWN QUIETLY

1. Squeeze the stomach to get at the last drops of air; this might mean you have to bend over slightly to squeeze it all out.

LESSON 9 – VIBRATO

1. That you're not working hard enough with your stomach.

LESSON 10 – XTREME FINALE

1. Your bum.